MADPO3T

PO3TRYVENT Before I Self Destruct

MADPO3T
DREAM IMAGINE EXPRESS

First published by ALEX MURDOCK 2026

Third edition

ISBN: 9781068267123

This book was professionally typeset on Reedsy.
Find out more at reedsy.com

Contents

Preface

The premise of this edition is rooted in a simple, Machiavellian truth: to delay an action that must be taken today is to give away your advantage. For the author, this collection represents overdue action.

Po3try Vent: Before I Self-Destruct serves as a psychological and literary release valve. It explores the tension between staying in a stagnant environment and the urgent necessity of self-correction. The work suggests that our habits- and ultimately our identities- are formed in the moments we decide to stop waiting for a situation to expire and instead choose to move.

This is the writing of a creator who has recognised that sensitivity to one's surroundings is not a weakness, but a catalyst for growth. It is a candid look at the transition from potential to execution.

Books By Alex Murdock

Publications:

Poetry Journal: Dream.Imagine.Express

Po3tryJournal: Growing Pains

Short story series:

Into the Abyss Volume 1, 2 and 3

Into the Abyss box set

Po3tryVent: Ramblings of a madman

Po3tryVent: Chaotic Ramblings

All available on Amazon
Author Copies on personal Website: www.dien.uk

1

ONE

One

Destructive Tendencies: Act 1

Feed the machine

Sore-picking like a picnic,
so much to overcome one may get sick.
All hailing with hands, 'Waiter! My order is sickness for one!'

Self-proclaimed as sickle-cells in my bones.
They jitter, a tectonic emitter, succumb to cave under pressure.

If growth is the matter, why do you stutter?

If expression is the process, why do you write with a negative reminisce?

Earth twist, withering as I fall back to the mist.

A cross-breed between a need to succeed and a need to breathe.

Can you see us?

Hidden betwixt the crab-like tree, perfect symmetry.
Even our chains feel the need to feed, on our flesh and bones if needs be.

Food for the many, platelet currencies.

I have to get it, with urgency, for needs are many.

Driven in turmoil, it maintains the affliction,
the rancid in my eyes, so when life spoils, I was never on the tidy side.

A safety net of incremental pride, telling tales of my darkest nights,
esteemed by ego.

Though it wavers, while it tries to fly,

little did it know, it was grounded, and never to take flight.

Ego's religion

The moments come like cronies, besmirched my nerves,
creasing torments like compressed bones.

Pressing through as though I'm carrying the ills for you.

Jesus in pieces, grinding my existence,
thus, not long until it goes missing.

Temperature increasing so essence disintegrate,
as my mind goes distant.

Snapping snapping, between what has taken place and is about to happen.

The world is trending in my phantom heaven,
processing my scary reminisce while forcing me to hurl and twist.

A juggernaut through my tender times,
they're draped and dragged through savagery.

Maniacal as I cut through fury, working a knife through my strife,
then fall back tired.

A cushion in mind, content in my death,
forgiveness and knowledge that I have tried.

A shark with my takes as they cut and bite.

Smooth to my fright, like adding sugar cane and liquorish to my plight.

Drinking my resolve as though they were solvents, no longer content to be dormant.

My esteem is groomed for heights, hanging from my ego's claws, extra sharp.

My tendencies like laws, so my policy is to study the crooked.

Tamely watching dormant, developing a lack of hope,
  forever caged, but no one knows.

Sick World

Refining my ways, observing cultural runs, like ancestral destructive plays.

Societal stampedes, a chronological growing tree of tyranny.

Telling tales of the times and the many turmoils.

While we stand aside or hitch a ride on the capitalistic brain tree,
that never meant any good to me or any.

A possessive entity, with the need to see clearly.

I sit as a witness to the in-grown doctrine, like a toenail that is yellow and malnourished.

Telling tales of the chains that broke, the times that cried,
but not for the cause of our sakes.

It was all for nought!

Mere efforts to debate as plates with brittle takes.

Earth in a primitive state, no good to me.

To have me blinded by blissfully, ignorance over eyes that fold.

To gain over time like cysts that breathe.

I'm in need of less flashing lights that distracts might,
causing an epileptic bite.

Connecting lines like a family tree.

Yet no more growth to take my life to a higher place.

My sunshine cries in dismay, while witnessing my predicament.

Thoughts wither in condensation.

I find myself lacking the glow-of-ray,
  that once upon a time that would spray the cobwebs away.

I see clearly the monsters that await, such was my ontology.

Relying on this cracked plate to feed the values of chaos,
  so my cells can continue to breathe.

Watching as my eyes percolate.

Smoke fumes as my mind no longer pontificates.

Methane remains for my courage lingers in the ethos,

Delusive.

No way to condense.

My environment is consistently strange as a pendulum of period swings.

Revolution is blurry-eyed so I'm seeking balance from the dormant side.

Tweaking a ride from a scary mind.
  Screaming beyond as a crow in flight.

Motivation is deranged.

Reflection brought forth vertical decay, surmising I could no longer stand the pain.

Wilting for more lifting.
   Smitten with poison to this day.

A world of your imagination

To cultivate in the premise, I'm stricken by your mere contemplation.

I possess the discipline to make fodder of experience,
tethered by various memories.

I proceed with insistence through times that are kindred,
an echoing chime of my cosmic lines.

To go beyond.

Stepping out of reality that are driven by my inclinations, to share my experience.

Conquest-like periods where I see myriads.

Shedding light on the crevices, unbeknownst, if you choose to notice.

The scope of art with a twist, a mad scientist that went wild,
primed to dive, in the onset of survive.

To look upon the universe as I climb.

Experience on the inside.

A telescope that I provide, slides that glide,
enclosed pondering, I've yet to acknowledge with sight.

The dream of colours,
they ride, run wild, like animals on the inside,
never to take a break, they never even tried.

Stick a pin to pause, as I run back in time to the periods I described.

A momentary pause is nothing but a sigh,
  they confide in my subconscious, which is known to creep when I'm tired.

Sometimes they punish the scale like I have no balance,
  splash, like a whale inside.

Equilibrium in a fight, my ship tipping over like the Kraken had made a child.

Beastly cold as I attempt to feed my smiles.

One day I will grow big from the ego and pride I provide.

Claws that a lion would try to hide,
  I'm flippant with the propensity to fight.

A sinking boat so time to wave goodbye,
  down in the deep blue, there you will find my life,
  permitted by the goggles, over googly eyes.

A scientist with a cooler side,
  waving from the colder nights.

I'm all seeing;
  omniscience.

Though, that's not me; simply the god-like being that resides,
  timidly revealing my civil side.

It may have got a little bumpy,
  I hope you don't mind.

An unstable seed that made a plant,
they suck the reason from my mind through a branch,
enabling roots to breathe out loud, to populate and sing and shout,
express their take on life,
congregating with a passion in a crowd.

The ultimate zest in my chest, I can feel them coming out.

Making a mess while birthing words.

Watching them making chaos as I speak out.

Word antics, driven from the roots.

Dirty brutes, wishing I had them in silence, stuck on mute,
but it was too late.

A blanket-take, to witness my vision in life,
unmuted.

II

TWO

Two

Destructive Tendencies: Act 2

Word Scientist

  Chopping word-trees in my sleep, deforestation.

It hurts every time, epiphany; chest-aching.

Jittery from a bird's eye and a vision from the brew I'm making.

Barley-words like gas cakes, they quake on the plate,
  then crumble like crooked pavements.

Deranged sense, perplexed by the staring.

Jumping from pavement, to cravings,
  like an Alsatian.

Juxtapose from lessons to wins, like learning.

Curly fries with the tides,
  stroking the cerebral,
  as they make their way in,
  another day in dismay,
  if I don't make the words sing.

Stick a pin;
  as they excrement,
  showing the dirty side of life, like Cavemen.

High-grade type of days, keep them coming.

No other ways to paint,
  dirty teeth with extra greenery,
  colour coordinated with HD scenery,
  mind mould lead to infected capillaries.

A double-vision, an epileptic with the blinding.

Corruption, on the verge of a grin,
   gnashers, clicking-clicking.

Ready-take-task, waiting for the go-ahead,
   just say when.

Electric Spill

Is time the ever-growing seed?

Driven in the need to be.

Fighting for the right to be me.

To unravel like an autumn tree.

A simile in the vicinity,
they tether to my unfriendly times until it no longer has means to breathe.

A sacrifice if it means the end of it.

An enticing debacle, with a hint of corrosive at the knee.

Timidly, I tell my story,
though hidden at the depth,
I'm stained with drippings of 'unapologetically.'

Destined to be rich by the day as a money tree,
driven by the greens,
they hang to my metaphors like leaves.

Tired of trying,
step forth into the beyond like I'm out of time.

Silly chimes, they thought I knew not of my worth.

At present, watching these rhymes,
composed and dripping red with a trickling effect,
brewed for the course like running blood.

Aged with depth for only then am I fine.

I get better with a hint of kind.

Night like the vision.

Written to the stars, the milkiest stage.

Transmitting radio waves ahead.

Useful Instincts while treading the crooked conductive rail-ways.

If only you knew and all it took was a look underneath,
then you would see my myelin-sheath.

Superconductors, protecting my brain- matter-meat.

Sewing Lines

Chaos like greens, feeding the mean.

Fodder like a beam, a nuclear dream.

Superman on carnage, with the need to accomplish, tongue twist,
persist-in the reminisce, reality- reflect all the same, ergo synonymous.

Geronimo-on the page, taking centre stage.

Time to wake the pain from bed to create word threads,
through my mindless-head, giving breath to my mental takes.

In times of jittery I commence to paint between the lines.

Make-manic-make-sense,
lack of breath,
like-man on meth.

Any-minute- I could lose my head,
word-explosives.

In a moment, I'm dead.

Hoping, nobody noticed, until life-bill is paid;
resurrection made.

I'm back,
breathing again.

I'm treading journey, but praying never too heavy,
I do my best to keep being fed.

I was bred in moments, rebirth made,
a yearn to be of service, giving back, through these words,
they over-create, have me in bed, like 'damn that's craze,'
yet I relate.

A prisoner of the moment,
I resonate,
I ruminate,
swimming in remnants that life would never be the same.

In need of a muse, the only one I can find,
the god inside, willing to ride,
through uncanny tides.

Through the strife of life, until life goes calm and the feeling is warm.

Periods grow to be controlling.

A mirrored message- 'let the future be mine,' storm be fine,
seamless is time, stars align,
revolution starts with doing, creating more jewels,
sentence sews chaos, reap more lines.

Not new to this

Dusting off knees, filled with subject matter,
creative with a motive, and extra cannon fodder.

Explosive tendencies, yet building mane,
ready to erupt like a congested brain.

But then it tames.

Checking my neck- rate while climbing the grim of life,
away from strife.

A millisecond carries potential as a drowning incremental.

A volcano like spring, nocturnal reflection,
showing imperfections,
sleeping with the spirits,
sipping on venom,
patience while effects subside.

Dormant tides, a burn with every try.

Criminal moments, mixed like pie.

To the moon by light, gasoline energy,
deep in pores, waiting for time, overwhelmed by brightness.

From throat to the stomach as I proceed to feed,
eating with a team of dreams.

No off days, so my team can dream.

Prognosis- osmosis, confirmed through the process.

Expectant in time to produce an identical vision of what growth is.

The tales will pay, everyday as a marathon headache,
running if but another day.
only then perhaps;
I'll be okay.

III

THREE

Three

Destructive Tendencies: Act 3

Can you see me?

Life in the fast lane,
blurry vision.

Picking at your soul,
consensus;
integrity.

Testing, testing,
extra stress, for days that are senseless.

Muddy waters, earthly solvent,
selective ignorance, hoping for bliss.

Time is a bullhorn, screaming your shortcomings,
while your unconscious makes straw-man arguments.

The ghost runner, I make the ghosts so I can run from them,
nobody knows but they keep me on my toes, my guilty secret.

Admittedly, a cycle effect, enacting in affect.

By design- a class act,
anxiety as fuel that keeps the blood awake.

Earth grunts, body stunts,
life clings to a slim, a brittle cultivation,
such was hope.

Once in a while it throws me aid, though timid.

Perhaps a strong rope with a hint of shade.

A medicinal trade that gives relief to the teeth,
grated in excess, while gripping for relief.

Ghost-like ships, hovering above secret juice,
giving a sense of superbness to my shadow as the black panther in space.
A Wakanda affect, 'yibambe,' the ultimate mantra like a secret vent.

Look around and you would notice,
a hint of hope, but nobody knows this.

Yet I can sense a stench, sour from the body like an expired smell.

Speaking to the darkest trees, growth with the smoke inside of me.

Can you see my gallery?

Ghosts hang like human bones out of my closet,
upside down like awkward crows,
about to fall and smash like pottery.

Exercising my demons, amicably, seldom gritting teeth,
triple extensions with feet.

In and out of the soul like a genie in a bottle,
a decrepit imagery, brittle forms moving without legs,
grotesque as they undress, I see it now.

A beautiful compilation, witnessing all my flaws.

What shine is mine?

Convoluted, uprooted,
friendly clouds no longer exist.

All I ever wanted was mine, consistently, to find my silver lining.

Earl-with-Greys, through the days.

Tender dismay, tranquil sheets to my cleats.

I would wake up with a viper betwixt my teeth,
surrounded by white like calcium treats.

Trapped and echo-bound, I bounce and bounce,
here to there intact with a crown.

A hemispheric plague, bamboozled by ideals,
excited by the thought of potential,
but never finding profound growth.

Through the smoke I'm constantly probing,
leaving me swiveling, like a shovel.

Six- feet facing down in the dirt,
never climbing the limits into the brightness above,
where the sun is compound and the signs align,
the confines of the mind comes forth,
exasperating in tales of what I found.

The greatest climb like sweet and sour tethers;
one of a kind.

Colours with an incline, to smile,

to multiply and to tell tales of a finer life,
floating, knowing soon I will no longer be earthbound.

Then came the time, gripping in the dark of the mind,
demonic in my approach at first I found,
but that was just me,
'brain-splaining' like a mind-tree.

watching from the smoke while sabotaging me,
a steadfast image, authentic with a sublime, like a prehistoric shine.

Attempt to capture was futile for what's to be was already mine.

Can't stop the smoke, can't stop the grind.

A light with a mission I'm destined to shine,
to glimmer in the glamour,
in the makeup of my own define.

Elusive dreams

The pounding sound of consternation,
so I let the words spill,
from the furthest crevices of my soul, 'I,'
had to let the world know.

Hell's mouth had opened whole,
to the root of our dreams.

No longer could I let my imagination stand just to feel.

The amicable calm in a stance as a referee.

To swim in doubt was not for me,
nor for you or any.

Looking beyond the great valley,
seeing the shadows awaiting my fall.

Universal knowledge, I've been on a tumbling journey,
yearning.

An attempt to discern, but never learning what to seek,
I've not yet gained the ability to see.

As I waited, I was displeased, uneasy,
faltering betwixt the chaos and vulnerability,
checking for myself as only I can save me.

A crucifix, with my elusive fix,
pondering upon the great beyond.

Teetering between, to peek in or abscond.

Afraid of what it might say,
 no presence of a friendly spirit,
 perhaps nonexistent,
 all existing was a destructiveness in my DNA.

The crows in teams,
 cringing as they scream,
 amazing,
 lame yet tame,
 they knew my name.

Word Brew

Word-brew, drink it then give it a minute,
now 'brainsplaining.'

Word precipitates like it's raining,
pouring like I forgot to stop the maiming.

The mental fluent with extra fluid.

Streaming with extra patience,
for it takes time to get such precision.

Simultaneous as the verse erupts,
Can you see us?

Flip flopping like an elder rocking,
hitting the floor with thunderstorm,
don't be alarmed,
it's just me knocking.

Earth cracks when I relax.

A light match with the extra pack.

The sprinkle in the winter,
appearing like they're anti-social.

Tinkering with my future.

I was born in the bosom of time,
the temporal manger.

The major with pleasure,
with ouu and awe,
as the straw-man when he felt his heart.

Pulsating,
bi-polar from the brew I'm making.

Words with eyes;
ergo criss-crossing.

Dirty plates feeding on raw.

A mental patient, living sabotage,
like I'm swimming with the crabs,
dirty sex got the world packing extra swabs.

Crazy and deranged, in this day and age,
nothing strange.

Laxatives have my intestines in rage.

Thus pardon me,
blame my word-diarrhea for the dirty page.

IV

FOUR

Four

Destructive Tendencies: Act 4

Time to shine

Cauterised, time coagulant,
soothing to the wound,
let the pain pass, I'll be fine soon.

Time broom, though taking its toll on the soul.

Deep breath in distress,
attention to the moment,
while cooking the ultimate chaos.

I was bred for this.

My untimely chimes reiterate as an echo,
as insistence,
to desist in and out of reminiscence,
but pain knows no bounds,
ergo- timeless.

Destined to go with the flow, until the day my bones turned to smoke,
my burns forget the need to choke.

I seek to live between my unpurified lines,
while curtailing their sounds behind the curtains.

Perplexing my subliminal nature that has me in a phase of puzzles.

Seeking to find ways to make you relate,
so no need to never-mind,
for we align like the most frank of times,
where the crows crawl to the surface,
at the least expected periods.

Telling of our dire and grime, the ultimate slime,
to then drop and dribble, fall from grace,
starting again as I reconvene with my rocky climb.

Curtailing my words to resemble expensive, like the greatest tithes,
kingly treasures, to prevent me from undermining my plight.

The ultimate try, where I confide in the conscious,
keeping my distance from sporadic mental underbelly of the unconscious.

I don't know trust, yet I remain,
smitten in past like mystic stains.

I only know the prompt, to clean the process,
to accomplish as the obsessive.

Task like a drone, to carry pounds.

Weighted exterior, no pressure,
a long time to wait, no leisure,
just a grind away, it mattered.

Ambitions to shine,
thus, I seek.

To take flight

Humbleness in bravado lines,
risky are the signs that depicted visions that you're mine.

Thrilling, lovers' religion,
crumbling amidst a blinking eye.

The sight of our potential and might,
from a crawl to a fly.

At the beginning, our initiation was like a solar flare, dispersing.

A kite seeking bird's eye, it was I, but then it was us,
a sinking synchronised.

Twice as blue, at sea seeking float,
crumbling as a broken pie.

No us, just I,
sitting with a dire plight.

Word fire

Down the rabbit hole we go, slip and fall, shed your soul.

snake skin anchored on a pole.

Barbed-wire, inkling, wrinkling your attire,
or merely crow, to scare away the little sense that you know.

No need for sense when crazy works.

Never mind your sanity, the forbidden tree,
cool if it makes you feel, only a crime when there's accountability.

A slip of the sleeve, then my name is leave.

Intercept begets an anchored pole.

The shovel digs until dirt swallows me whole up to my nostril.

I grow fatigued, it's engulfing me, taking away my will to breathe.

To grind for the sake of need, no wants in my vicinity.

Survival-like moments, picture wear and tear,
wrapped in cloth constantly.

Hidden in the fabric are my faculties,
showing sight of torments that only takes.

Atonement so I can be free,
so no need to return to comfort glee.

Seeking the groove of life with a smile,
  till death.

Shed away the torments, they remain but mere remnants,
  of times I dare not relent.

A crooked scent,
  clicking at my finger like incense.

Burning from the stem, waiting for a croak and spill,
  to alleviate the daggers from the traits that infiltrate my will,
  to abstain from the cranes that fill,
  and so my mind goes on search,
  to find resolve.

Lord knows I need solvents to tend to the spine,
  to cleanse memories like cotton that layers like cakes of dust over time,
  the likes that would have me dying on the inside.

Slowly confiding in the sickle-cells that reside,
  the friendly toxins that fight,
  unwilling to bear fruit to fight what's mine, once upon a time, until now.

Killing part of myself, to let the rest live,
  concepts so alien it felt grotesque.

Simply trying, moments like tides,
  growing sicker, every wave that climbs.

Tidal with a fight,
  I need context for strength, to keep morale.

Word-levies to incoming tides.

Gasoline spark that overrides,
  word-fires, an onomatopoeic flicker;
  with a hint of sigh.

A smile that a cry would catalyse,
  the soul could feel my heat like pyroman.

Painting even if I'm tired,
  I smile watching the words as they cry.

Emotional faculties, a raging bull that hides in the dark.

More than meets the eye, red that makes me quiet,
  being aware of shadows is sensing my pilot,
  they reach out their hands, to seduce my flight,
  but they couldn't make a sound,
  as the pain subsides.

Jekyll and Hyde, my gruesome pride.
  The words took a moment of silence, and all went quiet.

Grime is the way

Schizophrenic is the word.

Mindless like an ulcer and a thousand flying suicidal birds.

Crippling for crumbs, and crusts that has me dogmatic.

Never say quit, and so I juxtapose to grabbing.

Crabs in a barrel, now I'm 'illmatic.'

Excess extremes- I need gastric.

By-passing senses, like my DNA is demented.

Chromosomes on reload, but 'mum's' the word, Shhhh.

I can hear terror as the wind whistles so graphic, doing back-flips.

The pain got me feeling vibrations I dare not transmit.

Mode on depraved, extra pennies for the days that my mind is aided to rest.

Freedom is the way.

A martyr,
I'll never pay.

V

FIVE

Five

Destructive Tendencies: Act 5

Triumphant in the moment

Cool to be calm and collected.

Hard to the touch as though steel elected,
for stone may chip or erode,
bones may fracture from the cold.

So much ice running through my veins,
I'm paranoid prone.

Convinced that I may catch a virus,
or internals may shatter, making mal-functionality a factor.

Yet we stay the course,
through the eye of the storm.

Opportunities standing at the door,
hinting to 'take me home,'
a mirage of the warmest embrace,
there was nothing but icy space.

Iceberg idle,
Medusa syndrome,
one touch I could turn to stone.

The heart need not be,
the eyes do not need to see,
for life decrees there is a price to pay,
to be who we're meant to be.

I give my last every day,
to keep on paving the way.

Destiny awaits,
  for my plight to remain in pursuit.

If not, then at least for another day.

The underworld Ferryman,
  another life has span,
  so I reached out to take my payment;
  solace and satisfaction.

A triumph in a period,
  it was the only way to initiate my ascension.

Cracking like hydrogen,
  I relish in the path that anoints me.

The holy grail to my persistence,
  the snail trials,
  setting precedence for my future, a form of insurance.

No matter how hard I run,
  I could never force what's to come,
  and so the present remains dominant,
  until I'm worthy,
  for I'm not yet privy to the timing.

Stuck in the present,
  running forward with faith in hand,
  doing to prevent the past reoccurring for the things I don't want.

Balance restored.

Chilling inside

Chilling like a villain, thrilling in the moment.

Chroming in atonement,
where torments hit like grown men.

I have respect for the syllables,
they crawl through my paws,
requesting movement to pause.

I'm growing nauseous,
no running from growing,
gems like crumbs,
grabbing for the smallness,
placating my state,
I'm compelled to pay attention.

No such thing as lacking when you're leading,
waving bye to the weakness.

Staying in my lane yet swerving,
to never stay dormant,
for the sake of my calling.

I stay in the moment,
could never entertain the crumbling, destiny awaits.

Only one destination,
so I kept moving forward as stopping was not an option.

Lots of winning,

fighting for the right to breathe,
the facets of my being,
the follicles of my aspiration,
pouring on the inside.

The blood comes running,
then commenced the creating, amassing.

The periods keep coming,
I dare not miss it.

My words like spies,
eyes on all.

Word-ravens,
with crow features,
chimaera-like with wings.

Keeping my eyes on the prize,
comfort in discomfort,
I never miss.

Never distant, I refuse to loosen rope.

The flow may slow,
maybe even pause,
seldom, they come and go,
thus, they're seasonal.

An ability to intercept them,
a vibration, I receive it all,
with nonchalance.

Monumental keys that express private jokes,
life with a smile,
feeling on a high,
caressing esoteric tides,
perplexing my nice.

Lean with the passion

Composed like the image on pause.

The prickled rose,
causing headaches or runny nose.

Word-sickness, causing remission.

They ruminate,
commencing enlightenment.

The vultures that flock, to my corps when sickness takes place.

My relentless makes the daunting never overshadow my laughter rate.

My goofy makes my sighs reiterate,
taking off as flies or fish smells from a dirty plate.

I stand as the funky, amidst a dirty place.

To dream so vividly, then watch it come to fruition.

A vision, so I spend my days painting,
remaining, surrounded by colours so no way out.

To the crust and up with strong foundations,
a must with guts, curtailing my expressions.

To never hold back, I keep on making,
embracing change like a revolution.

Switching betwixt the times like a chameleon,

the thoughts come ticking,
like a clock that never sleeps.

I'm on a mission,
turning and churning, with my premise.

Gifted with sight; Simon says- giveth- word vision.

Slip through the cracks of reality, like word- missing.

Breaking matter apart have my diction in a schism.

Thoughts on tunnel vision,
poised through the noise,
smitten smitten.

A jailbird doing a bid, like 'look what I did!'

The world is looking like 'lord, forgive him.'

VI

SIX

Six

Destructive Tendencies: Act 6

Inverted Excursion

Creating inverted inflation,
  to foreign heights.

Infinite fight for the light, to take flight with my sight.

To paint words that fly like kites,
  taking off above and beyond.

The moon on man,
  a wordsmith with lead crown,
  sounds are renowned,
  to take the town for an extra round.

The gut stimulant,
  it takes a toll on the stomach,
  careful, ingesting makes one prone to throwing up.

A hiccup as we criss-cross.
  Earl with the swirl until I get lost.

Seeking moonlight to lead the way,
  a broom life like mop and grey.

Witchery could never succeed,
  words-flock wands in the palm of hands, word-wizardry.

It's all on me,
  ambitions to soar,
  even, behind the curtains,
  semi with the swift- like I was born inverted.

Inadvertently, sometimes I seek expression,
sweat to the palm of my hands, words come with glee,
hit the head like a log from a tree,
eyes searching for context.

I stand as the inverted, falling to the ground like this is buffoonery,
extra vert on the pile of smiles,
yet I let it be.

My chaos still speaks for me,
fragmented from ears to eyes.

Blood drain,
weeping with pride,
to take the mantle to inverted heights.

A sigh, to never hear my rhythmic cries.

Words come sweet like lies,
a puzzle that taxes the mind.

A readied spine,
to cultivate and fly.

Seldom words come with crime,
I do my time like the most diligent and kind.

Reaping between the meaning, so extra sewing,
never let sabotage fall between my seeds,
thus, graceful growth,
pulling weeds in my sleep,
thus extra mowing.

Yawning like the cow at dawning,
  telling myself I'm never tired like strawmen,
  then create straw-words for the birds,
  a reward for always feeling my arguments.

One with the chaos as I reminisce,
  watching birds flock to take an inverted piss.

Layered type of day

The need to fix a line.

A time loop, I'm in constant rewind,
polishing the moments so they could shine.

The telling of tales;
I look to bear witness, then proceed to leave them behind.

A sudden shift in the spine,
proceeding towards the cliff to climb.

I dare not look beyond,
for the journeys come like cliffs that hang.

Serenading;
I can hear their echoes in time.

Incongruence, an open frequency,
leading to my undoing, unless I tread carefully.

What's for you may not be for me,
but with compromise,
we could show each other the way.

No such word as stay,
a circle is a constant unless referenced with change.

Light infinity,
so let us shine in the moments,
then commence to brightness every day,
be distant from our dismay.

Elastic potential, stretching words with brainless takes,
practicing ways to show and tell about where I've been.

Growth in the moment,
bear witness while I turn grey.

Amidst memories like tooth decay,
presenting imperfections, I may need a cold spray.

Icy are the moments,
providing shivers like a northern day,
that comes with polar ways,
tweaking between the making,
watching as I rain on clay,
making a statement,
a colour play, like a rainbow day.

Belly-full-on dismay,
burping to excrete excitement,
then grasping in the air.

I wish you could stay,
but that's another story for another day.

A type of May

In a strange space, deranged yet with choice,
poised with criminal essence.

Ambitions to dominate, annihilate; the past.

A choice to proliferate thoughts in mind, with a clean slate.

Streaming, a world pool of black has me swimming,
rumination was the only way, getting in your feelings,
bearing witness to the thoughts I create,
see me in your vision,
convinced of the monster in the shade.

The moments paved,
pen-like-dulum as they sway,
between the two facials,
tombstone or icy face.

Thoughts are so cold,
periods leave an icy trace,
so, you can follow me, and the thoughts that leave me fazed.

No choice but to double-glaze through my ways,
for when I exhale, my surroundings melt in the moments like dames,
stuck watching a beautiful shame,
gripping to the days like a maim.

The unforgettable times,
now I'm thanking the stars my mind is trained,
thick-skinned, no more inked skin paying homage to the pain,
feeling the need to subconsciously abstain.

I merely call a spade a spade,
  embracing my time as merely a grumpy phase,
  in an icy place.

Torment comes like secret keys,
  hidden betwixt lineage.

The middle-man, like center stage,
  early rage had me stuck on a single page.

Surroundings, showing the likes of a cage,
  burning eyes, like a solar flare.

Existential crisis, creeping like a ghostly place,
  I can let slip a sigh but never breathe.

I could only express to the world after I've translated,
  showing my projections like a forensic case.

Bloody matter in eyes,
  I murdered the place.

An extra trained eye to see my pain,
  such is what it takes.

A primal hand to the chest like a Lion's mane.

Battle scars, thus, I'm never tamed,
  it's a fact, I can't reverse, it's too late.

A hunter, using my words as bait,
  writing words to make you jump,
  as I contemplate.

Word-concentrate,
  every day they pile like germs on a plate,
  persistent workings as solvent,
  picture scene as mace in the face.

VII

SEVEN

Seven

Destructive Tendencies: Act 7

Wherever life takes us

Soul-slip and torn,
regeneration is pending, a reptilian in the making,
the ultimate snakeskin.

Deep within the follicles of trauma,
my wounds grow warmer,
I blow sweet breeze to their ear;
my way of keeping them dormant.

I placate my spirit,
hopefully smile might re-emerge.

The lessons are fixed so my will can keep going.

An in-grown tooth, I'm home-grown,
but plagued by the unknown,
the undiscovered that cause bruises,
or forgotten memories of the spirit, that are less conditional.

The missing piece,
I grow with offensive teeth,
wisdom diffusing from my cleats,
my vibrancy oscillates when I'm in need.

No need for pride,
just wait till the pain subsides,
no need for hide, when the bones creak inside.

The petroleum to my torment,
the oxygen to my growing,
lessons keep on coming,

we congregate at the crossroads.

I keep on going, no need for a full stop,
when the journey keeps showing a path.

A constant reaping, yet ever sewing,
the shadow keeps on howling,
too many days in a void, feeling foolish as a clown,
but refusing to belittle where my feet had tread.

Symptoms of ulcers,
telling truth despite my moments of relent,
leaving me senseless amidst sense,
milliseconds, then I proceed to the trench.

Life with sore ears,
so I see with eyes to give context,
got to share intent,
until the time is right to show invest,
find me at the front,
with sharp words,
strict with the mind,
a prophet of the road.

Evolving with the times

Painting in the lane, close to dormant.

The crevice-like moments, many years, almost drove me insane.

Petty in arrangements, volatile to the naked eye,
many sighs, the verge of an outcry,
like a window through the mind.

The passive piles,
debating the spiel, a shock to the soul,
like steel, I feel, cold.

A running so remote at times it's hard to stay composed,
through the armoury made to refrain from the many ills,
threatening to remain in the subconscious.

I grow obnoxious with a whiff then a sneeze,
hand to trees,
leaning for the ultimate appease,
for nature knew the way,
though, I could never stay.

Mental threading away from surrender,
thus, in and out of tradition I would sway.

Iron on- man,
meat in the pan,
absorbing the world,
morphing until I expand.

Ever in dismay,

clinging to my day,
a face that tremors, irking my tooth decay.

The brew that sprays,
provoking revelations,
faith applied, I lead with belief that I will be okay.

I take pride in undoing my undermining,
the very lining that threatens to calcify my spine,
unrefining my silver shine, judging me,
for I never stood for the sun.

The cream cries to the top,
a constant that I wish to dust off my compass with a mental mop.

Reaping growth from sewing, thus, the sweetest crops.

Phantom smiles, proven instrumental,
incremental, discarding sweet and sensual.

I stay tuned to the periods, they carry scent-like fruitful rhymes,
layered with pockets of time,
infiltrating my psyche, taking me high.

I would be adrift in periods I knew not that I possess,
making a mess with the sweetest chaos,
visions of memories with explosive motives.

A time-bomb adrift in space,
floating, remote to face.

I knew no choice to elude their submissive cries,
until it was too late, for they tell the sweetest lies,

seeking my untimely demise,
I stay wise,
amidst the smoke.

Better with time

Let the clarity approximate gracefully,
lord knows I need a lot for my faculties.

Rub my eyes and scrub my teeth.

Fabric ripped and torn,
earth-worn,
discarding timidity,
giant hands to the skies,
voluntarily,
with a stretch as I reach over to grasp for me,
beyond reality.

They say it starts in the mind,
I polish my constant, feeding myself mentally,
grotesque with trample as monsters' feet.

A shuffling mannequin,
if I feel these lines recline from honesty,
purposeful and amicably,
they serve in time,
temporal mastery.

A remnant of my untimely chimes,
when the words proceed to climb.

Ants with resolve,
strength in numbers,
they take over my endeavours.

A rabbit hole with optic treasures,

telescopic leverage,
a hawk with eyes,
excess stimulation and unique pleasures.

The past like a mass I can't help but weigh.

I bore witness to semblances of a baby with a plea, 'please let me stay,'
begging to remain in the mental cradle,
but it wasn't the way.

I'm in need of a new day,
but it was too late,
rested my temporal potential in a moment with less dismay.

Let there be funk

The chapters creep between the pages,
  from an early age.

All that took to pride was what resides inside.

Never run and hide when it comes to the confines.

To confide in the gruelling tides that protect me from hanging dry.

Never take sail and run away from the turmoil times.

Always up for a fight but never to prove my might.

They say stand but never plant,
  stick and move with a hint of gallivant.

In the trance, my words come through like reprimands,
  the extra trance that makes my blood dance.

Vibrations through the hands,
  they make my features take to stand, at a pause like plants.

Driven to a halt like pendulums that hang like vaults.

Immovable objects met unstoppable force,
  zero velocity screaming halt.

Like a bad referee with the similes,
  they placate my faith,
  then send for me when faculties are in need.

My brain keeps, running into the need to excrete,
poetry-vent of the mind with the beat of the feet.

kicking to the forefront until my secret feat is complete.

Reaping with heat, a reaper, a swordsman until I'm complete.

Cut and change until the moment leaves me less deranged,
though I can see, the page still shivers while taking a seat,
just another day for the pen's dark-spread to complete.

Smiles are like sweets, they stick to my cheeks,
when the damage is done, I breathe,
now I feel complete.

I would take a seat on a volcano like it's nothing to me,
ready my chaos and smoke screens,
in a stance about to take my word feed.

Venting for days if it means my soul is complete,
clipping at my words like I'm damned through witchery,
but, that's not me.

This is mere word wizardry.
the type that sticks to my hind,
a man who takes to heights like I've grown a full moon inside.

Jumping in the air like Superman about to take flight,
but it was just my words showing their claustrophobic side.

Thus I'm inclined, to find the remnants that nullify my mind,
so I can sleep away the questions until another time,
where the inclines of mental tax can be unpacked,

I take time to brew these lines,
so they may not impact my ego and pride.

A sewage line is a terrible waste,
they placate my space.

Sometimes I run like diarrhea with amazing grace,
hurling for days,
I would bear witness but never phased,
watching like what's the big idea,
I'm merely showing my funky face.

still never phased,
wondering why everybody's mind is stuck in a dirty place.

VIII

EIGHT

Eight

Destructive Tendencies: Act 8

Supreme dream

A supreme dream trying to stay lean.

Lifting so muscles stay trim.

Controlled aggression, but face stay mean.

On a mission to win, so extra scheming.

In the motion of pouring, thus, excess potion.

Logically stroking, a homage to what will come.

Life's conundrum, make my bones go numb.

Discipline thus stricken to not fall like crumbs,
instead rise to heights like a voice with helium,
take off like spirits amidst rum.

A result of pure word manipulation,
no chaser, so pretty potent, have me clinging to ribs,
hailing lungs to pause as I ponder betwixt the steering and levitation.

Yet still sipping to stay supple, thus no quitting,
a result of the putrid pain, so extra saline.

Contemplating gateways give headaches, so sipping morphine.

Never tamed, wild like the life of a stray,
gnashers speaking words that hangs like wisdom teeth.

A holy treat as the rain washes pain,

porous, dripping through the cleats,
then wishing for the days to repeat,
groundhog comes to mind,
but we've never been one of a kind,
so never mind.

Extra trying,
bringing forth the tides.

The scene betwixt the curtain,
showing strands of myself that I wished to evolve.

Seeking greatness through progress,
humility of where I've been,
still bewildered and soul searching, for it was just the beginning.

True is the way

Hard dealing of late.

Absent-minded through periods, finding 'difficult' but 'no-relate'.

Like a mind mould about to mutate,
   make me see red until it overtakes.

An occasion with fear that permeates,
   and so the toning of the torments comes with a certain face,
   with a crime taste,
   Joker with the laughter, chuckling faith.

Smiling as I'm destined to turn the page,
   yawning in the mornings like I'm always late.

Patience for the sunshine to clean my case,
   where I no longer consider the shortcomings of yesterday.

Writing to create is like a life with pace,
   unusual as I'm used to running in the absence of grace,
   living as though a marathon is the way.

Creating has me pondering an eclipse,
   impression in my mentions, like the destined existential.

Lord knows there's insurmountable tests, so dare not embrace inept.

To tell these stories that cut deep like the slit of the wrist,
   soothing pain, sugary like liquor cane.

Painting every time like 'tomorrow is not promised.'

Every day operates like the last,
  sticking to the task, like I'm gifted with a rifle in a mud bath.

No time to laugh,
  but I take my time to endure, for sunshine barely entails what I craft.

Telling the truth with a brute,
  sometimes I wish my mind were on mute.

No lies in my surmise.

No cries for these ties,
  they were meant to be like special keys,
  unlocking taboo thoughts like forbidden memories.

No option to leave,
  thus I spread my circle, inviting them in like my terrible kids,
  the skeleton family tree.

A telling that pleads as the witness who reminisces about me,
  ever-best are the doubting, to come after me if I were ever to shy away.

No room for friendly,
  for the lines may blur, in the sand that time wants to withstand,
  telling of my maniacal feats across the land,
  it was decreed, approval stamped,
  let the legacy stand.

Chilling with the times,
  Earth and the truth shall burst if I ever retire.

To never be sired from these chimes,
  refrain from crying in my outline,

for art is the way, thus no need to sigh,
live by the truth so never die by the lie.

A mouthful if I ever find the need to be kind.

Well deserved, should I proceed?

As insulin, gratitude should come with a spike,
letting the destiny bells ring with a hint of fire,
sending time to the grave with a bang.

Can you see me?

I call this ordainment that grows on trees,
hence why there's no need to try.

Time of passage

Crafting, getting crafty in the dark,
at my best when I'm creating my own spark.

Like wedding bells in the park,
a tree so tall, collapses in the lonesome.
Did it really fall?

I shed these veins, in any terrain.

Discipline have me smitten, witnessing the stain of my dragging remains,
bloody vision with a hint of strain,
but if the world was to carry on, there was reason for my call,
to share what's mine, it begets a certain high.

Picture me as eyeballs recline,
driven at times by the third eye,
they aid to shed my extra layers,
thus parts of me I'm prone to leave behind.

The ultimate climb, life with the loudest sighs,
when you can only imagine what you left behind,
driven to live in a grave in the dark,
if wings were never willed so I could fly.

A child with a sight, every time is right,
it was meant, stricken to the elements,
my mind signifies, it will all make sense in time.

Treading on the lines of relent, can't hold back now,
it wouldn't coincide.

To the stage we go, to share the misfortunes of the cocks and crows.

The familiars, knowing you'll relate,
you know, I know.

Life of late, eager to dominate,
but never taking anything for granted,
so the universe can get used to my ways.

A culture with a pen,
my tribalism is coded with rebellion,
take it to the furthest capacity.

To the dark ages, when there is no more me,
these words to the Chesser Peak.

Birds, carry blessings and curses,
to the wilderness amidst the meek,
word-treat.

IX

NINE

Nine

Destructive Tendencies: Act 9

Beautiful Chaos

I share kinship with the gods,
semblances of commonality.

The go-ahead with a nod, to smile at thee,
there commenced a path.

Needless to say, it was set in stone,
I decided.

To never waver as we look beyond the stars,
into the misty I sway, and beyond,
into the great abyss, betwixt the darkness,
where our thoughts were set on rocky hills.

Our aura danced in the unknown,
for to go beyond one only has to breathe,
if one chose to dare,
there isn't much out of the realm of the imagination.

Dedication, taking me places.

An owl on a step, with an excessive wingspan,
dare to reminisce, on the ever-bliss,
the timeless courage that rises to heights,
no test could withstand.

If only the world could grow above melancholy,
there you would find me, with a bird called Timeless.

Stroking the cerebral,
wishing for the days my dreams take to fruition.

To take off with grace, leaving me mindless,
  in a beautiful mess, wishing I would remain at my best.

To grasp omniscience,
  the undiscovered,
  a secret garden.

Camouflaged by paradoxical confines,
  embellishing my ambitions, with intentions to capture my mind.

Wouldn't that be an endeavour?

At the epicentre, there lies inspiration,
  the hidden gem one was willing to die for.

Brain flu

Bird flu, leaving hinting clues,
losing my compass as the mind loses screws.

Invading, to have my brain loose,
that makes the toes bruised and scorched,
encouraging my fall.

Dripped and draped through the rules,
my sense of directions in disarray,
once was a need to soar, turned upside down,
pointing towards my fall, little did I know, until I crashed and burned.

I could never delay redemption,
for night is followed by another day,
time passes like temporal paddles,
compulsion to usher and coerce my psyche to forget yesterday.

The treachery hangs like garments,
a habitual in-growing pain,
concepts so daunting,
equilibrium has never been the same.

Influential with the words, screaming to run away.

I proceed to express what I feel with meaning,
a page that stands for something, what could be more real?

Difficult moments have meaning to me.

Making solutions like my last meal,
the hard feel sometimes as it enters the gullet.

The brain protrudes to the lining of the stomach,
to tell lies about my epithelial cries.

Distraction of the sweet and sour type of noise,
for cells works in alignment,
they are quick to surmise substances that dictate my demise.

Earthly cries,
if solutions don't carry antidotes;
I misspoke,
these words I speak won't leave the throat,
my cries won't land remote.

Alien in a giant,
the balloon like tyrant,
all air in my nightmares,
the ones that left me breathless,
heaving to the point of senseless.

Nitro for the microbes, contracted from my untimely throne.

A mortal spawn, grown on Earth,
seeing comets and asteroids,
the extra pounds would fall to the ground.

Shoulder shielded and protected,
regimented with confidence.

A brazen voice,
telling tales of my legendary plight,
word cries.

At the end of my fever

What is the meaning of abundance when we thrive in poverty?

Remedial and lacklustre.

The intangible periods,
  leaves me quaking and sullied.

The fragmented torments like chaos in a hurry.

A nomb to the warmth,
  so cold I can feel the ice making its way to my soul.

A solvent through the soil,
  even on water I would float.

Never to alleviate the toll that weighs,
  but to be dethroned by the chrome, I refuse.

The tons hang long from the dome.

I drag my head like a king without lineage or code,
  lost in the absence of beauty and once was,
  instincts was all I knew.

Friends of a note,
  I would sketch complexities of the inner workings,
  perched on the front of the inner functions,
  slipping through periods of painful whispers, in my DNA.

Exploring the treachery at present.

Darkness meets me at the level of the eye,
my mind at any minute is about to break as a dam,
like the damned.

It was all perfect but for a scream,
until it commenced.

At the end of its completion,
I was no more.

Witnessing the end,
the milliseconds as I await the process,
to my further demise.

I started to look forward to the time I had transcended,
let the elements make sense,
let forever be my recompense.

X

TEN

Ten

Destructive Tendencies: Act 10

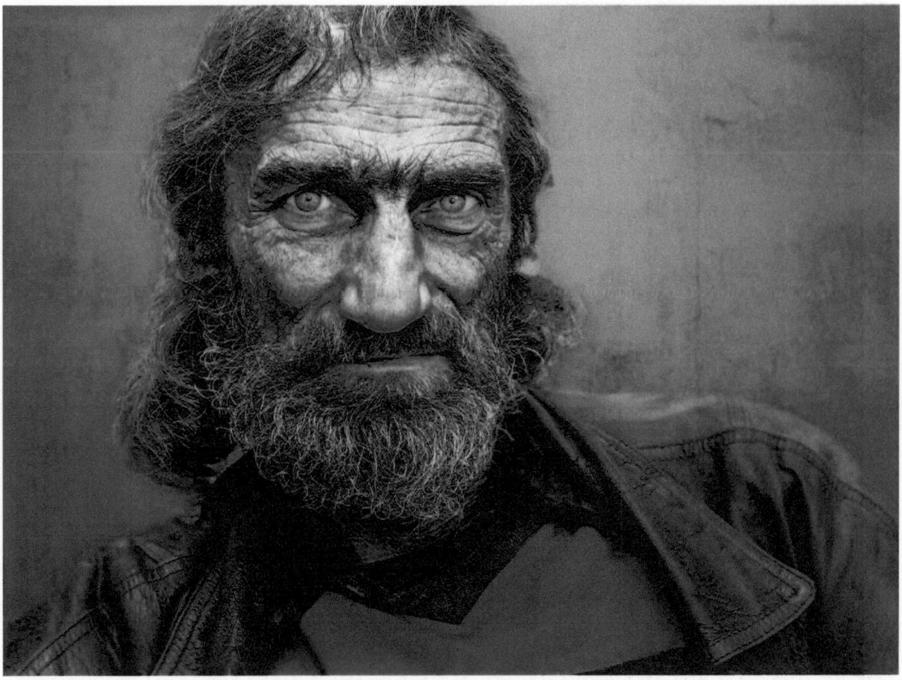

Straight shooter

I would tell myself, 'It is time for your daily dose,'
then go about pouring ice in my veins,
piercing through these clothes,
freezing persona accomplished, mode on cold.

So cool, one breath too hard, I might be prone to freeze my soul,
I take these chances despite knowing what I know.

A watered snake in a glass with no chaser,
although, these words are immortal, so no fear.

Talking in the dark camouflaged like the slickest crows,
owl defences, ready to orate these words.

Speaking while reaching betwixt the fix as I take my oath,
take my code to the heights of the skies to continue this road.

The immortal path that will follow my every word, note by note,
telling of the journey and the grime, like relics that stand to form.

shouting, but for the grace of me, I will never lose to any storm.

I take the catbird seat in the middle of the eye,
then sigh, witnessing their faces, knowing they were misinformed.

The secret sermon that makes you want to repent, then fly,
to the moon and back through the third eye.

The genius that sits between us, we are what the world seeks to be,
no need for teach, for I've already written my destiny.

Looking beyond the sea, into the abyss in awe as it was just me.

Deeper than water while secretly scheming to part the Red Sea,
  speak with the fishes, while viruses and bacteria take a knee.

Pledge allegiance to the eminence that makes no sense,
  a fool with the tool that is prone to scurry and shoot a mouthful,
  leave you breathless within the realm of the unconscious.

Word-tosis, all that exists is a wish you had not doubt my request.

All hail the praying mantis prone to throw split hairs and semantics,
  the frantics to my tongue twist have my neck crooked and slightly twisted.

Rehabbing nerves, until the days I see the world that one dares every day to exist,
  where these rhymes remain sullied in time, like a poor man with his last dime.

It takes time, but I knew I'll be fine,
  the last of my kind as it relates to faith.

I'm inclined, to steer the way no matter the day,
  like the Titanic one must go down with the ship.

Shooting from the hip if my word potential slips,
  then walk with a limp, making me prone to kick and slip,
  knee-jerk with my ill-words, like an army as they disperse,
  have me in an uproar, for I've ascended to a new universe.

Monster in the shade

To conjure the conqueror,
an intriguing hemi.

A menace with a premise.

The king of monsters.

The only person who can tame me is my mother,
nature's mouthpiece.

I'm a demigod!

Ego grows like monuments,
thus, I do my best to practice relent,
for the darkness comes like tides.

Making my mark wherever pain resides,
senses go so senseless that I make tired grow tired.

Maniacal on steroids.

Fire with a plight.

To grow to heights,
I look down, convinced I've already died.

Freedom so painful my blood like gasoline inside,
ignition like a spark from the outside.

Churning for a burning, thus I'm exploding like a fight,
though the more I try, the more rapid chaos grows inside.

As my mind bleeds my darkness grows.

An army at my fingertips as a result.

A bloody mess if my mind goes into the abyss.

A train wreck if the brain makes my vision go blurry.

Scheming with a scurry,
embracing monstrous ideals in a hurry.

Stepping with a flurry,
about to take a leap of faith into my next fury,
fiery flames borne of maims.

I see in my mind I'm headless,
in a daunting mess,
trying to find the life of forgiveness,
for destruction sat too comfortably, with me,
for far too many years.

What makes it worse is the world did not know what it was doing.

The world is mine,
from the tip of its toe to the head of the spine.

Although I'm inclined to drive, the whole planet, over the end of the cliff,
smashing everything to oblivion,
even the things I see as my prize.

If ever in a mess, I'll figure out a way to rewind time,
when my thoughts come with the mission,
I'll tell myself to tell me to never mind.

XI

ELEVEN

Eleven

Destructive Tendencies: Act 11

Let the mind speak

All I need is a time and a place,
demanding grace,
commanding space.

Thinking like taste,
thoughts like paste,
they hang long in the tooth like moments I trace.

Silly periods with context,
dangerous torments got me feeling I'm next,
but here I am, no complex.

Turning every opportune into my best fit,
sullied with the right,
but prepping with the left,
so when I trip, I fall to my next best fit.

A conflict like cats and dogs,
the antagonist, the disassembled alchemist.

Still searching for the perfect experience,
a better for the palate, where you grow with atonement.

All it took was a whiff of what I seek to repent,
for the life of self, I wish to be brainless,
spilling with potential like a hemorrhage.

A stainless, poking my head less,
waiting for the cerebral drainage,
hanging from the mouth, like Jordan's tongue,
word sprung.

The torments have been lingering on for so long.

Potential, I'm elemental with the life lesson credentials.

Credibility of what life has meant for me,
  the brain is compelling me, to keep telling a candid plea.

Never hold back for the life of me,
  for there is no solvent for the parched birds within these words,
  they fly like high swords at noon,
  bloody as the red disperse.

Batman sullied in time,
  do the crime, and these words will find you.

Changing with faith, but I'll be fine soon,
  to be kind until I find tomb.

Word flies betwixt the gloom,
  got me facing a raw deal.

Crooked like it was meant to be,
  a rhyming lung with ambitions to pop with glee.

No way to display what you mean to me,
  to speak with glee,
  no small feat,
  life has never been nice ever since the family tree.

Watching in the dormant like 'come get me,'
  fiery, looking at gasoline like 'come ignite me,'

Free from melancholy,

I was never able to do the trifling with a face like honest.

Emily rose with the crows,
leaving me with demonic scars,
have me speaking in tongues like isms and schisms,
word-exorcism.

The elephant in the room

Political subliminal,
   criminals perpetrating Seminoles, of old.

Gorilla warfare with weapons they tote,
   some say somewhat, but prone to fold.

Trickery grows the roads that glorify the untold.

Nothing new under the sun,
   the historical diarrhea, they run.

Time and time again.

Protruding through the natural,
   denatured like strange,
   monsters from another world.

Clay face until my skin unfolds,
   naysayers jumping to the white like umpires,
   proceeding with intentions and crooked words,
   'what have you done?'

Cruising to abscond,
   alphabetical, so numerical;
   although such uniformity,
   had never meant any good to me.

What about my brother?

My sisterly family tree?

Although lacking faith, she herself would turn from me,
then make potent a demise designed for me, if I dare tell with real.

The truth, though still from the heart, like love still lives.

I wish we could find better ways to console thee.

A life that withstood the storms,
I stand with heat, betwixt the bosom that runs with lava.

Poetry venting for thee, the truth no matter how brute,
our family's affairs of late,
telling of times through these rhymes.

To turn from the shuns of society,
denaturing the black family tree.

To hurl from grace, it hangs like acid in the chest, fully,
to protest at the grotesque of the world we are tied to, yours sincere-fully.

No class for the mess as we grow dusty like the Loch- Ness,
monsters are us for we drew with inc,
turning from black to pink,
for we rush from T.V to sink to throw the baggage of toxins.

We are worse off than the previous children,
and even worse off in pondering,
of our previous-previous children's-children.

XII

TWELVE

Twelve

Destructive Tendencies: Act 12

Bitter is the way

Train wreck like my faculties are coming at me.

A turmoil spill with a glee.

Hopping from the trenches like a jumping spree,
I'm stuck catching bullets for the life of me.

Triumphantly,
wishing you would call me to safety.

No space for free,
thus I'm painting with grace to the fullest,
in the onset of my pain wreck.

Watching it all until morning,
all I want is a perfect explanation,
the logic to your dictation.

Cringing if the matrix takes from me,
dwindling in a disarray spree,
habitual with the spasm, like polar feet.

Turning to the north like 'teach me,'
shedding soul in the south for the love of me.

The only way was to give, so that I could breathe,
my life liveth if it be the death of me.

My crown tree keeps ticking comfortably,
but for my compass to be centered,
I had always sought to be me.

Thus, I grind these lines,
in the best version of my essence,
poetry-vent type of mental,
with a hint of tea,
call me cerasee.

The more bitter it gets, the more I see,
you never meant any good for me.

So, I stand at a distant, ingratiating perspective,
I surmised it was never meant to be,
if your resolve is to put a dent in me.

A king to a lion, a peculiar dichotomy,
despite, replicating myself until I'm complete.

Manipulating like science,
Dexter with the traps in my laboratory.

Frankenstein with the words,
scheming about making my next Mary Shelly.

The ponder is the crux of creativity,
there's no face for these rhymes,
they run like a family tree.

Until the death of me,
they tell tales even if it means to hell with me.

Objectively,
that's where I aim to be,
telling the sweetest stories.

Tickling gracefully,
  like a case study.

I make way like waiters with entrees,
  they make space for me,
  to breathe away fatigue,
  and doubt I don't need,
  just the need to succeed,
  to carry this crown with ease.

The silly maims that drain,
  causing excess bloodstains,
  corrosive with the colours,
  getting on my nerves.

Getting used to the pain,
  continuous with the lame,
  every day feels like another day,
  dispersing lines,
  until they leave me numb,
  or take my breathe away.

Just my words

The barrels run low, scarce, making it an easy scrape.

No way to drown out this misery, a conduit, receiving all I can take.

Buffoonery has an extra vibration to its laughter rate,
trying not to relate, for I dare not bring myself to a lower state.

The cerebral telling my sinus to respond in kind- but maybe at a later date,
where the defects of the crabs may not be privy to our clear like faith.

Implementing screening for the mental's sake.

Thus, when I sneeze, there is no need for the mistrust of actions my gut makes.

Soothing with a plight that's losing, into the unknown got me crowing.

Until I'm writhing in the tithing while my lethal bile envelopes in crates,
causing the devising of my worst takes.

I think we relate,
my intentions were never to resonate, to the trolling of the tame, and melancholic lames.

They threaten my laughter rate,
my assignment to liberate.

No longer do I wonder about what fear makes,
I no longer seek to relate.

One day it may be destined to take me as the universe ordained, timing with my demising like demon plates.

Poison in the veins, so my vibrations congregate.

To the process of swallowing whole, stuck on demon time,
cyclically tainting my surmise, to know what's right.

Just grime after grime- wheezing like darkness with a slime.

The prime to my evil I never wanted to acknowledge,
in a constant of repelling like 'maybe another time.'

The moments are not mine for I don't recognise,
they no longer represented my side,
could never see myself as a fiend of such poor lines,
depicting a narrative that would add shadow to my own trait, like crying,
a dark circle around my eye.

I couldn't allow pride to have me on groundhog, a constant rewind.

Stuck in a day like a bird cage for the ages,
my senses goes missing, I could not perceive it.

Ridiculous hence why I could never receive it,
thankful it was never mine and so I will never retrieve it.

Onwards and forward,
no backwards, just my word.

XIII

THIRTEEN

Thirteen

Destructive Tendencies: Act 13

The good fight

An accomplice to my own treachery at times,
I find these lines redefine my insides.

Remnants drip in sips from my confines,
though the piles of daunting ever wanting to make me sigh,
taking to the highs of the skies, I dare to take flight,
but these were mere delusions of the misleading type.

Feeding a series of misdeeds,
to overthrow the values that make me try,
so no more highs, just lows, birthed with wings but too heavy to fly,
too levied to be light, the ultimate glass ceiling, I have a tree inside.

Growing roots to feet yet attempting to tread air, despite the fight,
but for the life of me I could never bear to retire.

Sired to take the plight to the limelight,
feed me instructions, like algorithms, forever scarred, brain chipped and pinned.

Sticking to the surface until I see my way in, a machine with presence, felt with skin,
prolific with a felt tip pen as my mind grows ever more serene.

How else could I look beyond the great sins?

They take to my pride like ants showing their schizophrenic side,
engulfing my every rise, I'd never again be in a feel-good night,
just the light that sprays rays, on the untimely plagues, looking to catch me without a spirit inside.

I never fight for the days that are still mine,
doing well to disarm my contemplation, of the finite times,
the loveless rhymes wants me in a mess, thus I play chess inside.

I'm never in a mess, just organised chaos that repels disingenuous allies,
so, the-sicker cells could never mutate my every being without a fight,
for I would never survive, without the will to summon and throw relics like dynamite.

My demons see me coming, like why do I even try?
Thus I multiply, by swallowing a mirror through mouth,
seeing daunting thoughts, coming to fruition like future tides.

Hard paper with ideals and values, to pierce the calcified like mental lies,
making it rain with precipitation, I take pride in my cleansing.

I'm unrelenting, but at night I keep to the dark,
it sticks to my hind, like monsters, a figurative impasse,
leading to a scuffle, raising stakes, seldom times I discovered vampires on the inside.

Trying for life if only for a good night,
waiting for the pressure, like 'yes that's about right,'
I think it's about that time to say my goodbyes.

Heart like Candid

Crab-tree that hangs like monkeys, constantly trailing from branch to branch.

The existential crisis of herd mentality is like mental paralysis,
once you no longer cultivate to emancipate to go in faith.

Blinded vision, lord forgive him, he did not know it was missing.

The brainwaves from the slave days have him smitten,
telling of times he thought no longer existed,
yet one look clearly still showed him a victim.

The prism that he had written had him playing in curls like girls,
'brainism' is crashing with precision, like it was written,
in the confines of his designs,
the ultimate genetic readmission.

Taking from my family to give back to 'the have lots',
driven by the poor man's decision,
blood ridden with blood-clots,
segway to make him a paraplegic.

The mentality have me in a place like 'I'm bedridden,'
no word or action, to change or impact what my family's missing,
to enhance what young man is feeling.

Changing his diaper, a shot to the spine has his functions in a schism,
a ricochet trying to make his way to work one morning,
another hater is locked away,
while my brother's- Mom- Aunt- Sister- Shekisha feeds him porridge.

The tube life of strife, for my family still mourns for life-less irresponsible

decisions,
 to almost take a life- only thing worse is failing while trying,
 whether my brother sits, lies awake, or sleeps, I can't tell the difference.

No reminiscence for the times that exist,
 they persist through the periods one can only depict,
 poverty of the mind is a terrible taste,
 worse of the mental dribbles from food leaves a terrible trace.

The politics are polluted,
 carnage runs between the damage done by the suited and booted,
 though their screw-face leaves no trace,
 and no point stating the place they show their criminal face,
 falling on deaf ears for their crimes will never hold case.

So grab her by the family tree, Trumping it up like candidly like it was meant to be,
 but 'shh,' tell no one this is just between you and me,
 and if anybody finds out,
 who will they believe, you or me?

XIV

FOURTEEN

Fourteen

Destructive Tendencies: Act 14

That's Just Me

Talking to the walls like my mind is stuck in solitary,
until they talk back, have me feeling ghostly.

I can sense the cerebral remnants dying to tell my stories,
pouring like maggots on these words, sometimes extra gory.

The sickle slime and lime, but they paint a journey so refined,
the painful and the unkind, like 'you really know me.'

I've had to take the time to elevate from the dungeons, no dragon story,
yet breathing fires for they cater for the flames of the inner me.

No story without a mountain to climb,
no refinement without the unbecoming of one's own self, being unkind,
the 'must I remind you,' to refine the liking of the inner child,
to cater for the inner confines,
where I can tell these failures and try with a smile.

Gracefully, let sunshine fester more in my plight frequently,
so no more throwing petroleum fluid,
where the pesticides of the past shall fester lovingly,
bonding with his story.

I make piles of smiles my story,
the stand for something, or fall for anything.

Why not stand for me?

The roads get tough, too tough to give up on self,
we want to win, despite the onset of walking pins, the type that grinds,
where death echoes but duty calls, for my times were destined to be.

I see the pictures connect when I hit my objective, gracefully,
never miss, I perish the day, never let it be me,
where I could never tell these words from a place of candid.

An alcoholic, I stay in remembrance of my crooked times, depicting me,
telling of the hellish wounds that reside on the insides, got me heated like high noon tea,
but, it has got to be,
I can never abscond the work of my internal factory.

Healing through feelings, like 'is this really me?'

The reversing and evolving to my evolution, constantly.

Can you imagine the irony?

That's what I want for me.

Not one for do(s) and can't,
not for me,
honestly,
growing with pride humbly,
with an ego on an earthly tree,
coming with essence like 'yeah that's me.'

Speak truth to power, 'you feel me?'
I think that's me, logically,
in the absence of sense,
then it doesn't make sense,
honestly.

Training day

Sullied in time like I wrote my name on it,
echoes of the future tenses and passing dominants.

Telling these trinkets through the rhymes like I damned it,

The mind is like tony-tony in betwixt the cosmic matrimony,
a cross between the explosives and a terrible motive.

I come and go in time with a shape like bullets,
shooting for the stars, yes I'm gifted with ordainment,
to create the word solvents that echo through time like a torment.

Prickled breeze that leaves you phased as you hit ground-to-knees,
there's no telling when they're coming.

Brain-drops, I grab my word-mop.

Critically, sweeping through the runs like dormant.

Although I don't have to own it,
just leave my DNA on it.

Thus, X marks the spot,
it may take time but these lines will hit you in a moment.

Never tired, life of the enthusiast.

Never fired, I'm just flowing,
if ever feeling trapped I relax like sonnets.

At will, stay ready with implosive,

in sight of impedance like a frontal-lobe disease,
it may take some time but you'll get it in a moment.

The vent don't need praise, just a pen and a sheet,
sitting there writing about the world I see.

My imprints run deep, like kitchen sinks.

Runny eyes and extra sighs,
you may need a pliers and tissue when I'm enthused.

'Mos def,' I have extra flowing in the torment,
the spider sense that blesses when I'm present,
caution for the relent may be prone to leave a stench,
steady as it goes while the earth grows cold,
like the dinosaurs.

Never mind me, I'm just peeping what it's like if I'm on it,
tweaking in my sleep if these lines are short to feat,
so let me speak my piece and complete this moment.

Heatwave

To treat the canvas like a universe,
as my thoughts disperse, I know these thoughts will tell a story of the untold.

The special world where only the unique lens can depict,
to enlarge into a place everybody wants to see,
resonate in the belly like a treat,
then regurgitate to the world the standards we've yet to meet.

The times are crooked with callous chimes,
it endeavours my taste buds to be unkind.

Unsavoury are many things to me.

Leaders are not leaders anymore,
humans are rarely kind.

The carriage before the cart as the guilty before the innocent,
I remain dazed in relent waiting for the secret scent,
where the mind is prone to take aback, abashed upon the injustices.

The short list is a mind twist,
the forgotten has not forgotten about the turmoil times that still reside,
many men locked away eating porky pies,
terrible lies are the crooked ties that lead to many untimely demise.

Protect the women but punish the lies,
outliers are not sired thus if you try, to cause a man's demise and many feats in itself,
why isn't that a social cry?

T.V world to rule mankind,
technology and cosmetics.

Talks of the cosmos are things of the past,
feeling like Madmax,
nothing will last by the end of the periods we cease to exist.

To live is the challenge that sounds like a tricky concept,
hold on let it exist but for another second.

To live is to exist like a sheepish mind,
follow the droppings like 'ish,' the infected and carnage, nature's defiance,
they lead the forefront while still trying to find their spine.

There is no love anymore that exists in a vacuum,
elusively consumed like virus to a broom,
on guard for the witches to come home soon,
our world looks inflamed and heated like a pent up room,
heated heartache burn for we show no concern.

A blossom with an accelerated bloom,
soon to wither like Icarus, destined to fall back to humble beginnings soon,
wildlife in need of icing to prevent baking doom,
unrelenting is the definition of life,
destined to live with the blues.

To take the world into the dark spectrum,
the world is in an unconscious tantrum,
mental feel like it needs 'Selsun,'
for these white matters never did anything, for the heat it has received.

XV

FIFTEEN

Fifteen

Destructive Tendencies: Act 15

Cool to be

At present with pain and steadfast.

A splinter-cell through glass as I aim,
clinical moments, daring not to lose a classy embrace.

What would they make of my cruel take?

Excreting grace, in a vacuum, in black holes of space.

Ingesting cold, a forceful heave like trees on their knees.

Infectious roots, in life, no such thing as cute,
to have me on mute would be the ultimate suit.

Yet ego will forever have claws,
to maul through the skin like curtains meet paws,
have me crawling through the raw,
cutting through the unfiltered carnage like a brain saw.

Can't take these petty outliers,
playing in the circumference of art, like my soul has been sired.

To paint like the saint, ordained by the lord's sake.

My gremlins like shade's, frequency at a high rate,
I see them coming like a mummy, but I'm fast with my pace,
quick to enact my dissociation.

Never one like the life tree,
not to be seen as they napped me.

A trapped star, yet there lies synergy.

Energised to replicate, and rewind with symmetry,
  through my timelines like rhythmically.

My slime can no longer get to me,
  now in constant alignment, 'can't touch me,'
  sweet to the life, like sugary,
  we were never meant to live under siege.

Repetition on mission mode.

A business of growth like steroids seeking fertility.

Developing, through my untimely crimes like a cactus tree,
  a prickled touch, yet comfort.

A process through the rain and frost-bites that may get me.

Ice cold in a 'frozone.'

My resolve has grown to be crafty,
  never to return to factory,
  I'll forever be gone with the wind,
  like dust with wings,
  a stoic voice, while the face endures empathy's misery.

Disciplined Dream

There is lineage behind these dreams,
weighing over pounds,
thoughts with a mechanical oral drag.

A ton, rolling beyond periods.

A pause to jaws, thought of triage, traps like pyramids.

Trend-setting, reminiscent of heights of growth,
impact to the bones.

The unpredictable, living a life of the unknown.

Earth grown but unrestricted by a dirt throne.

I have ambitions to speak to the universe,
as my thoughts echo another baby is born.

A beckoning world with inner and outer worth,
the semi- circle, to my purple heart, an Emmy's worth,
drama with the dreamer's curse.

Telling about the light, but saw darkness first.

On the brink of convergence, working confines,
to transmute these infinity lines.

Bags intact with expression,
no feelings pressured to shed a verse,
or explode with a burst.

Never to corrupt imagination with a mortal case,
gifted with corpse, I have death running through my veins.

Vision so vivid, sweet to the taste,
running but never in vain,
cunning like bloody waters before it stains,
adapting to every vision, remaining cool, thus I precipitate.

Juxtapose to times that are unkind to the sweetest case,
but the shade is so cunning, always clinging to my bird vision.

I needed a rocket man,
hurling from my earthing like a socket man,
cooling to the bones with my extra tan,
croaking in the motion like a dolphin with extra hands.

A mad scientist in a bird cage,
driven to remain smitten until I take centre stage.

I swing to spread my wings in air,
out to the world, no haste.

Serene, I was never fazed,
I want you to relate so I could never fake.

A mastermind, cultivating to master prime,
time to get mine.

Telling the real with a cage appeal,
spoon feeding like stainless steel.

Showing untimely scars might ruin my mission,
a worthy sacrifice to elevate my bird vision.

THE END

A NOTE FROM THE PUBLISHER

MADPO3T

DREAM IMAGINE EXPRESS

Thank you for supporting this book. If you enjoyed it, please consider leaving a review on Amazon to help others find it too. **We Hate Errors.** We work hard to edit and proofread our books, but sometimes mistakes are missed. If you have spotted a typo or any error, please let us know, and we can amend it within hours. **Dreamimagineexpress@gmail.com**

www.ingramcontent.com/pod-product-compliance
Ingram Content Group UK Ltd.
Pitfield, Milton Keynes, MK11 3LW, UK
UKHW040232290926
15471UKWH00002B/148

9 781068 267123